D0055898

Rookie reader®

Joshua James Likes TRUCKS

By
Catherine
Petrie

Illustrated by
Joel Snyder

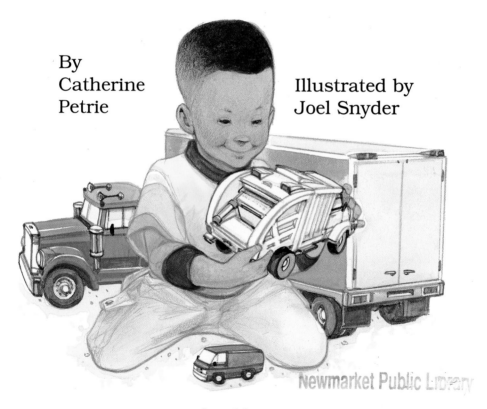

CHILDREN'S PRESS®
A Division of Grolier Publishing
New York London Hong Kong Sydney
Danbury, Connecticut

For Luke
—C.P.

READING CONSULTANTS
Linda Cornwell
Coordinator of School Quality and Professional Improvement
(Indiana State Teachers Association)

Katharine A. Kane
Education Consultant
(Retired, San Diego County Office of Education and San Diego State University)

Visit Children's Press® on the Internet at:
http://publishing.grolier.com

Library of Congress Cataloging-in-Publication Data
Petrie, Catherine.
  Joshua James likes trucks / written by Catherine Petrie ; illustrated by Joel Snyder.
      p. cm.—(A Rookie reader)
  Summary: Joshua James likes all kinds of trucks, big trucks, little trucks, trucks that go up, and trucks that go down.
  ISBN 0-516-21639-2 (lib. bdg.)   0-516-27000-1 (pbk.)
  [1. Trucks—Fiction.] I. Snyder, Joel, ill. II. Title. III. Series.
Pz7.P44677Jo 1999
[E]—dc21

                                                                            98-54222
                                                                            CIP
                                                                            AC

FEB 5 2000

GROLIER
PUBLISHING 1 2 3 4 5 6 7 8 9 10 R 08 07 06 05 04 03 02 01 00 99

Joshua James likes trucks.

Big trucks,

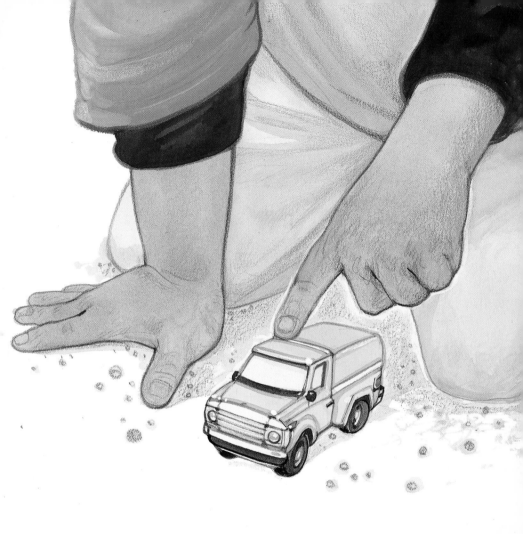

little trucks,

long trucks,

short trucks.

Joshua James just likes trucks!

9

Red trucks,

green trucks,

yellow trucks,

blue trucks.

Joshua James just likes trucks.

Trucks that go up.

18

Trucks that go down.

Trucks that go round and round.

Joshua James just likes trucks.

Word List (19 words)

and	Joshua	short
big	just	that
blue	likes	trucks
down	little	up
go	long	yellow
green	red	
James	round	

About the Author

Catherine Petrie is a reading specialist with a Master of Science degree in Reading. She taught reading in the public schools and her experience made her aware of the lack of material currently available for the emergent reader. Her creative use of a limited vocabulary based on high-frequency sight words, combined with the frequent repetition and rhyming word families, provide the emergent reader with a positive independent reading experience.

About the Illustrator

A graduate of The Rhode Island School of Design, Joel Snyder lives and works in his home in upstate New York. Having recently restored his 150-year-old Gothic Revival home, Joel does what he was born to do—fish, illustrate, and give lots of TLC to his young son, Adam.